Patio Daddy-O

Patio D

addy-O

'50s Recipes with a '90s Twist

Gideon Bosker, Karen Brooks,

and Leland and Crystal Payton

with Lisa Shara Hall

CHRONICLE BOOKS

SAN FRANCISCO

Introduction by Gideon Bosker.
Recipes by Karen Brooks and Lisa Shara Hall.
Photography and image archives by Leland
    and Crystal Payton.
Design by Reed Darmon.

Library of Congress Cataloging-in-Publication
Data:

Patio Daddy-O:'50s Recipes with a '90s
Twist/by Gideon Bosker, Karen Brooks, and
Leland and Crystal Payton
    p.   cm.
ISBN 0–8118–0871–8
1. Barbecue cookery.   I. Bosker, Gideon.
TX840.B3P38 1995
641.5'784'–dc20   95–21388
                    CIP

Printed in Hong Kong

Distributed in Canada by Raincoast Books
8680 Cambie Street
Vancouver, B.C. V6P 6M9

10 9 8 7 6 5 4 3 2 1

Chronicle Books
275 Fifth Street
San Francisco, CA 94103

Dedication

For Alan Fleishman,
a great dad whose love of life and
generosity of spirit inspire
everyone around him. And to the
memory of two loving fathers,
Martin Bosker and Joseph Levy.

Contents

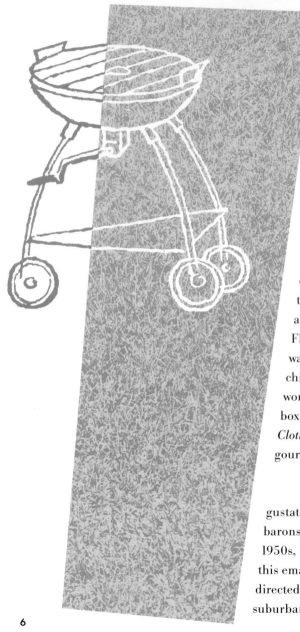

Introduction

This culinary *man*ifesto has been years in the making. For so many generations, our fathers, our fathers' fathers, and our fathers' fathers' fathers – and all the fathers back to Adam, for that matter – spent their lives as passive recipients of feminine culinary skills. But at some point during the quiet Eisenhower years, as nuclear families gathered around the grainy transmissions of a Zenith TV console to watch beatnik Maynard G. Krebs on the *Dobie Gillis Show*, this changed. In fact, it was over the backyard grill, steadied by the certainties of the Ozzie and Harriet decade, with skewers, Charcoal Wizard Lighter Fluid, and Worcestershire sauce in hand, that *Patio Daddy-O* was born. Under sunny skies, with red-winged blackbirds chirping, and children munching Oreo cookies, modern workingmen shed their roles as refrigerator vultures and ice-box scavengers, or as Robert Loeb, author of *A Wolf in Chef's Clothing* explains, they were freed from being "a parasitic gourmet forced to feed on the leftovers of female cookery."

Some men had long sought the opportunity to become gustatory eagles: to take their place as kings of the kitchen, barons of the bar, and maestros of the backyard feast. And the 1950s, more than any other period in modern history, facilitated this emancipation from culinary obscurity, at least as far as Daddy-directed cooking on the domestic front was concerned. Although suburban homes sprouting in Levittown, Skokie, and Shaker

Heights were equipped with all the kitchen conveniences anyone could have wished for, they also featured patio eating areas – never mind the dirty umbrellas that stayed out all winter – where, in the bosom of his family, the post-war American male could explore his epicurean talents.

Patio food of the fifties was like Prozac for the tongue and tummy. Uplifting in almost every respect, lawnside meals of this era kindle warm memories of full stomachs, two-parent families, and apparent emotional harmony. Who can forget those immensely satisfying, gut-filling meals of humble means? Hunks of watermelon, Kool-Aid, sweet corn, green Jell-O molds, and Oscar Meyer weiners would fall off soggy paper plates and tumble onto the grass, where they became either instant pet food or the buffet for an insect hootenanny, depending upon the sucrose content of the slippage. Sometimes no larger than ten feet square, the flagstone patio became the modern equivalent of the Neanderthal fire pit: a meeting ground where the raw, the savage, and the cooked came together in the service of family, chow, and masculine gastronomy. It was camp food with all the conveniences.

Patio dining, however, was not without its risks. No suburban household was immune to patio-based

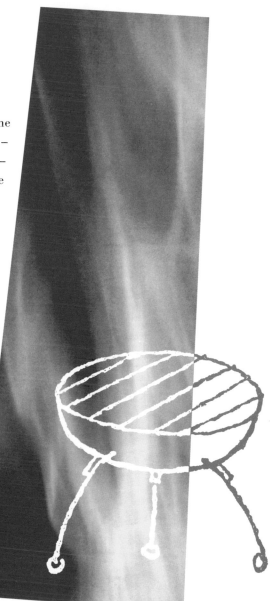

conflagrations of the culinary variety. Most of us can recall the treacherous, hair-singeing, backyard fire-dances our daddies executed in the name of grilled grub.

The road to self-immolation, patio-style, was never a pretty sight. More alarming, though, is just how predictable these backyard fireball follies were, and how often they occurred. We can remember them as if they had happened yesterday. First, our dads would direct parsimonious squirts of lighter fluid onto the coals, light a match, then silently pray for ignition. When this failed, as it almost always did, they would douse the dark nuggets with a steady waterfall of lighter fluid, desperately goosing the can to produce long, arched streams. Then a second match. As the coals caught, our fathers were suddenly transformed into fire dancers from Samoa. In their Born to Grill aprons – they should have read 'Born to *Be* Grilled' – patio daddy-o's would perform strange hops, skips, and jumps as they tried to dodge tongues of fire that leapt wildly out of the grill in search of the black, white, and red Charcoal Wizard cans they still clutched precariously in their hands. "Hot potato, two potato, three potato four. . . ."

Fireballs aside, when the man of the house donned his chef's apron, ignited the coals, and spanked his grill with a slab of T-bone, it was time for the woman of the house to step aside. After all, patio cooking was, for the man of the house, an act of profound symbolic importance. Discriminatory economic incentives in the 1950s drove women back into the home, where they became the primary bulwarks of gastronomic defense. Toiling in their linoleum kitchens, which were usually outfitted with the latest GE range and Hotpoint refrigerator, mothers nourished their families with devotion, while for the most part, men contributed little to day-to-day cooking chores. If bringing home the paycheck was a rather abstract exercise in family sustenance, then hands-on preparation of the patio meal was a concrete display of the father's biological role as provider.

And he made the best of it. The daddy-dominated, patio gastro-bash was an exercise in gustatory savoir-faire, in short, a ritual signifying the man's ability not only to bring home the bacon, but to cook it as well. With this in mind, *Patio Daddy-O* picks up where the 1950s left off. This book is intended to empower all men, and women too, in the art of fresh-air feasting, patio-style.

Although inspired by the preparations, techniques, and time-honored comestibles that made up mid-century outdoor cuisine, the recipes in *Patio Daddy-O* go one step farther. By adding a twist, spice, ingredient, dollop, or flavor here and there, we have attempted to bring '50s classics, from coleslaw and brownies to chili and barbecued chicken, into the '90s. Whether prepared in the backyard, on a rooftop, deckside, or on the front porch, these are recipes both novice and expert can prepare for friends and family.

The purposes, of course, are culinary enlightenment, benevolence, and to break down traditional culinary roles. Consider, for a moment, the scope that *Patio Daddy-O* cuisine can offer the enfranchised backyard chef. As Loeb explains, "The man of the house can shine as a host by being able to serve custom-made snacks and drinks, not factory-made ones. For state occasions, anniversaries, birthdays, Mother's Day, guilt, and appeasement days, he won't just be limited to flowers and mink. He'll be able to serve brunch or supper fit for a queen, and let her do the dishes for a change. It's a saving all around." So, step aside, Iron John. And welcome to the world of patio cuisine.

– G i d e o n   B o s k e r

Grilling Tips

Open-fire cooking was the backyard standard in the '50s; cookouts weren't cookouts without the barbeque. The taste and smoke that a real fire creates are unduplicated in more modern – electric or gas – appliances.

The type of charcoal grill is unimportant: You can even grill successfully on a grate in your fireplace. Don't get hung up on designer widgets. A grill is just a grill.

As for fuel, we like to use mesquite charcoal (not briquettes), although it does take longer to get to the coal stage and does spark when being lighted. If you prefer, use standard briquettes, lump charcoal, or hardwood.

We also like to use an electric wand starter to eliminate the need for lighter fluid. Try not to use pre-soaked briquettes, since they have the same chemical fumes as lighter fluid. A charcoal chimney is another handy device that bypasses nasty chemicals.

Always use more fuel than you think is necessary. However you get the flames going, don't even think about beginning to grill until the coals are coated with gray ash: Never cook over flames. To test the temperature of your fire, the coals will be red and covered by a thin coat of gray ash; for a medium-hot fire, the coals will have a faint red glow, and a thick coat of gray ash; for a low fire, no red glow should remain, only gray ash. To double check the temperature, hold your hand about 4 inches above the cooking surface: For a low fire, you should be able to leave your hand there for a count of 5 seconds; for a medium-hot fire, 3 to 4 seconds; for a hot fire, only a second or two.

Remember to give yourself enough time to get the coals ready: Start the fire 45 minutes ahead of cooking.

Paying all this time and attention to charcoal grilling is really worth it! Backyard food just doesn't taste like backyard food without it.

Chapter 1
Backyard

Classics

Let us celebrate here the icons of youth, the time-tested formulas for great gatherings of friends, the food-rations for growing, gawky adolescent bodies. These are the recipes to turn to when you have a prodigious hankering for those delicious, down-home, psyche-probing classic Americana foods.

1 Patio Daddy-O Burgers

2 Pink's Grill Chili

3 Slab-O-Fun Barbecued Meat Loaf

4 She-Devil Dogs

5 That Smokin' Lemon Chicken

6 Fabulous '50s Fried Chicken

Patio Daddy-O Burgers

Huge and juicy, these exuberant specimens have charred edges and a beefy perfume, all sizzling under cheesy goo. The secret is a cold ball of herbed butter placed in the center of the thick meat patty. As the burger cooks, the butter oozes throughout, creating a deeply flavored, moist interior. Pair these burgers with Spo-Dee-O-Dee Chips (page 75), sliced pickles, and cold beer. To make the hamburgers really special, grind the beef yourself in a meat grinder or food processor – the flavor is much fresher. Add a slice of roasted red pepper (see page 63) for extra punch.

Herb Butter
- 4 tablespoons unsalted butter at room temperature
- 1 tablespoon minced fresh parsley
- 1 tablespoon minced fresh basil or oregano
- Salt and freshly ground pepper to taste

- 3 pounds freshly ground round
- 6 slices Fontina cheese
- 6 split hamburger buns or other rolls

1. To make the herb butter: Place the ingredients in a blender or food processor and pulse until smooth. Transfer the mixture to a piece of plastic wrap. Roll into a log using the plastic wrap. Freeze until firm.

2. Prepare a fire in a charcoal grill (see page 10).

3. Divide the beef into 6 equal balls. Slice the

butter log into 6 slices. Bury 1 slice of butter in the center of each meatball. Flatten each ball into a patty about 1 inch thick.

4. When the coals are medium hot, place the burgers on the grill and cook for 5 minutes on one side. Flip the burgers over and cover each with a slice of cheese. Cook for 3 to 4 minutes, or until the cheese melts and the meat is medium rare. Cook a few minutes longer for medium or well-done burgers.

5. While the cheese is melting, place the buns, cut-side down, on the grill to lightly toast them. Place the burgers between the toasted buns and serve.

Makes 6 burgers

VARIATION: Substitute a different cheese for the Fontina, such as Swiss, Cheddar, or Havarti.

Pink's Grill Chili

T his all-day, brick-red brew, powered by dark beer and devilish chilies, has a flavor that will drive any chili aficionado crazy. It's beanless and a mouth-blaster, with chunks of steak buried in its deep-red depths. The recipe was the trademark of the dearly departed Pink's Grill in Oregon, owned by filmmaker and supreme retro cook Don Gronquist. Leftovers can be smothered over grilled hot dogs or folded into omelets.

- 4 pounds well-trimmed round steak
- 6 large garlic cloves
- 4 pounds coarsely ground hamburger meat
- 2 yellow onions, coarsely chopped
- 7 tablespoons good-quality chili powder
- 3 tablespoons ground cumin
- 6 teaspoons salt
- Two 14-1/2-ounce cans beef broth plus more as needed
- 6 dried California chilies
- 5 dried pasilla chilies
- 12 ounces dark Mexican beer plus more as needed
- 1 teaspoon dried oregano
- One 14-1/2-ounce can stewed tomatoes
- One 4-ounce can diced green chilies
- 2 tablespoons paprika
- Sour cream, chopped onion, and shredded Cheddar cheese for serving

1. Prepare a fire in a charcoal grill (see page 10). When the coals are medium hot, sear the steak for 30 to 45 seconds on each side, or just long enough to nicely blacken the outside. Let cool. (This step adds a great flavor to the chili, but can be eliminated by the shortcut-minded.)

2. Cube the steak and place in a heavy 10-quart pot. Press 4 of the garlic cloves through a garlic press and add to the pot. Add the hamburger meat, onions, chili powder, cumin, and salt and cook over high heat, stirring frequently, until the onions are translucent and the meat is browned, about 15 minutes. Reduce the heat to medium and cook for 1 hour, stirring occasionally. Add just enough beef broth for the liquid to come up to the top of the meat. Return the heat to

high and cook, stirring occasionally, until the broth cooks down to a glaze.

3. Trim both ends of the California and pasilla chilies and shake out the seeds. (Be careful not to touch your eyes when handling chilies.) With a sharp knife, slit the pods down one side at the seam so that the chilies can lie flat. Scrape out any remaining seeds.

4. Put the chilies in a large pot. Add enough water to cover the chilies by 3 inches. Boil for 30 minutes over high heat; the chilies will flavor the water and create a broth. Strain the chili broth through a sieve and set aside. Reserve the chilies and let them cool.

5. While the broth is cooking, dice the remaining 2 cloves of garlic. Place in a small saucepan along with the beer and the oregano. Bring to a boil, then reduce the heat to low and simmer until the beer takes on a dark green hue, about 3 minutes. Strain and reserve the broth.

6. Lay the chilies, skin-side down, on a clean work surface. Scrape out the soft membranes with a knife — it will look like thick chili paste — and set aside. Discard the skins.

7. In a blender, combine the chili paste with the stewed tomatoes, diced green chilies,

paprika, 1 cup of the reserved chili broth, and all of the reserved beer broth. Add to the pot of chili meat. Cook for 2 hours over medium-low heat, adding chili broth as needed to keep the mixture moist. The chili should be thick but moist when finished.

8. Ladle into bowls and serve hot with bowls of sour cream, onions, and cheese for topping. For a deeper flavor, refrigerate

overnight and reheat. (If the chili becomes too thick, thin it with beef broth or dark beer.)

Makes 5 to 6 quarts; serves 20

VARIATIONS: For a sweeter chili, increase the onions to 4. For a smoother texture, eliminate the steak and use a total of 8 pounds of hamburger. For an intriguing dark flavor, add 1/2 square (1/2 ounce) grated Baker's chocolate in step 7.

BE MODERN!

Slab-O-Fun Barbecued Meat Loaf

- 5 slices firm white bread, crusts removed
- 2 large eggs
- 3 tablespoons heavy cream
- 1 ¼ pounds ground round
- 12 ounces ground pork
- 4 drops Tabasco sauce
- 3 tablespoons grated fresh horseradish or water-packed horseradish
- 3 tablespoons minced onion
- Salt and freshly ground black pepper
- ¾ cup chili sauce, plus more for serving

When perfumed with horseradish, covered with a chunky chili sauce, and cooked over hot coals to absorb a sizzling charcoal flavor, meat loaf becomes an essential addition to the summer cooking repertoire. You may never want to bake meat loaf in a regular oven again. Serve with a mound of creamy mashed potatoes, Cheesy Drippin', Garlic Fumin' St. Louis Salad (page 72), and The Best Backyard Brownies You Ever Ate (page 86). But make sure you save enough meat loaf for sandwiches; it's terrific on balloon bread slathered with mayo .

1. Place the bread in a blender or food processor and grind to fine crumbs.

2. Transfer the crumbs to a large bowl. Beat in the eggs and cream, mixing well. Add the beef, pork, Tabasco sauce, horseradish, onion, salt, and pepper.

3. Shape the mixture into a smooth, rounded loaf and place on a rack on a shallow baking pan.

4. Prepare a fire in a charcoal grill (see page 10).

5. When the coals are medium hot, push them to one side of the grill. Place the pan with the meat loaf in the middle of the cooking rack. Cover the grill with the lid, open all the vents, and cook for 1 hour, adding additional coals halfway through.

6. Remove the lid, pour the chili sauce over the meat loaf to evenly cover, and replace the lid. Cook for 20 minutes more.

7. Serve with extra chili sauce on the side.

Serves 6

She-Devil Dogs

These hot dogs and beans are the quintessential lazy-day meal, but think beyond opening a can and heating. Think sci-fi. Think of the heat of a she-devil's eyes. Think about burying spicy sausage in home-simmered smoky sweet beans: a retro meal full of fire, fun, and flavor. For a variation, substitute juicy hot dogs (Hebrew Nationals or other kosher brands have great taste), or make the beans without meat. If you're feeling ambitious, whip up a batch of Back Shack Blueberry Corn Bread (page 78) and serve the warm squares on the side with honey and butter.

- 1 pound dried navy beans, soaked overnight in cold water
- 6 bacon slices, cut into small pieces
- 1 cup finely chopped onions
- 3 tablespoons sugar
- 2 tablespoons dry mustard
- ³/₄ teaspoon cayenne pepper
- 1 ¹/₂ cups dark molasses
- 3 tablespoons cider vinegar
- 2 cups tomato juice
- 1 cup water
- 6 spicy Italian sausages, cut into 1-inch lengths
- Salt to taste

1. Drain the soaked beans and place them in a large pot. Add fresh water to cover, cover the pot, and bring to a boil over high heat. Reduce the heat and simmer until the beans are tender, about 1 hour. Drain and set aside.

2. Preheat the oven to 250 degrees F.

3. Place the beans in a 3-quart casserole dish. Stir in the bacon, onions, sugar, mustard, cayenne, molasses, vinegar, tomato juice, and water.

4. Bake the beans for 4 hours, checking occasionally and adding water if necessary.

5. Add the sausage and cook another 40 minutes, or until the sauce is thick, the beans are tender but firm, and the sausage is thoroughly cooked. Season with salt.

Serves 6 to 8

21

That Smokin' Lemon Chicken

Forget about those high falutin convection ovens – you want a serious bird, a succulent bird, big and bronzed with a crackly skin and a smoky, lemony perfume. This one is a triumph of the grill: a whole chicken slow-roasted over hot coals to create that finger-lickin', crisp, and falling-apart essence of soul. The pure, simple flavors make this dish adaptable to all sorts of side-kicks, from Eat-Now Potato Salad (page 70) to Sweet Heat BBQ Coleslaw (page 74). For variety, add a few sprigs of any fresh herb to the body cavity.

- 1 roasting chicken, 4 to 5 pounds
- 2 lemons, each pricked 20 times with a fork or knife
- 3 tablespoons olive oil
- Salt and freshly ground black pepper to taste

1. Prepare a fire in a charcoal grill (see page 10).

2. Place the lemons inside the body cavity of the chicken. Truss the chicken with cotton string, tying its legs together securely. Rub the chicken with the olive oil and season inside and out with salt and pepper.

3. When the coals are medium hot, push them to one side; place a drip pan in the center of the fuel bed.

4. Place the chicken on the cooking rack over the drip pan. Cover the grill and open all the vents.

5. Cook the chicken for about 1 hour and 15 minutes, or until the juices run clear when a knife is inserted between the thigh and the breast; add a handful of additional coals halfway through the cooking time.

6. Transfer the chicken to a carving board and cover it loosely with foil. Let it stand for 10 minutes, then carve the bird into serving pieces.

Serves 4 to 6

Fabulous '50s Fried Chicken

Served hot or cold, crunchy fried chicken is the ultimate back-yard or picnic fare. Here's the classic treatment with a provocative cayenne snap. These boneless, skinless breasts are super crisp and pack a sassy bite. Make sure there's plenty of Eat-Now Potato Salad (page 70), Back Shack Blueberry Corn Bread (page 78), and squares of Big Daddy's Back Porch Chocolate Cake (page 82) for a perfect picnic.

- 2 cups milk
- 12 drops Tabasco sauce
- 6 boneless, skinless chicken breast halves
- 3 cups unbleached all-purpose flour
- 1 tablespoon cayenne pepper
- 1 tablespoon paprika
- About 3 cups vegetable oil
- Salt and freshly ground black pepper to taste

1. Combine the milk and Tabasco sauce in large bowl. Add the chicken, cover, and marinate at least 3 hours in the refrigerator.

2. Mix the flour, cayenne, salt, pepper, and paprika in a large bowl or a paper bag.

3. Bring the chicken to room temperature. Remove the chicken breasts from the milk one at a time. Shake off any excess liquid and toss a breast into the flour mixture to evenly coat it. Set aside and repeat the process until all the pieces are coated.

4. Pour the oil to a depth of 3 inches in a deep, heavy pot or deep-fryer large enough to accommodate the chicken without crowding. Heat the oil to 350 degrees F on a deep-fat thermometer, or until the oil is almost smoking.

5. Using tongs, place the coated breasts, skin-side down, in the hot oil. (Be careful—the oil can splatter.) Fry about 6 minutes on each side, or until a deep golden brown.

6. Drain well on paper towels before serving.

Serves 6

Smoke Gets

Chapter 2

In Your Eyes

The ecstasy of foods grilled or barbecued is usually expressed in animal sounds. People don't do much talking when they're gnawing on smoky ribs, juicy chicken, or sizzlin' seafood slathered with serious sauces. What you hear is the smacking of lips, the moans of pleasure after the first bite, and the sighs of satisfaction after the last.

1
Rock 'n' Rollin' BBQ Baby Back Ribs

2
Love That Kabob

3
Cracklin' Sugar-Charred
Cowboy Steak

4
Mondo Bongo BBQ Chicken

5
Piña Colada Shrimp

6
Grilled Tuna with Jamarama
Pineapple Relish

Rock 'n' Rollin' BBQ Baby

There are two kinds of barbecue eaters in the world (actually, a world of sub-genres exists within these two groups, but that's a different book): those who eat their ribs wet and those who like 'em dry. This recipe satisfies both camps, thereby preventing family feuds and fist fights. The ribs are marinated for a minimum of 5 hours in a coffee-fueled, chili-blasted barbecue paste. Slow-cooked over a low fire, they're all the smokier when soaked hickory chips are scattered among the coals. Chicago native and renowned ribs innovator David Estes serves them dry – these bones were meant for gnawing. Or, for wet-rib fans, baste the ribs with your favorite barbecue sauce during the last 5 minutes of cooking; serve additional sauce on the side. California and pasilla chili powders can be found in the Mexican food section of supermarkets or in Latino markets. If unavailable, substitute your favorite chili powder.

Back Ribs

Barbecue Paste
- 3 tablespoons ground cumin
- 2 tablespoons California chili powder
- 1 tablespoon pasilla chili powder
- 2 tablespoons ground thyme
- 1 1/2 tablespoons garlic powder
- 1 tablespoon ground celery seed
- 1 teaspoon ground ginger
- 1/8 teaspoon ground cloves
- 1 teaspoon black pepper
- 1 teaspoon salt
- 2 tablespoons packed brown sugar
- 1 1/2 cups very strong coffee
- 1 tablespoon Worcestershire sauce
- 2 tablespoons black molasses
- 1 1/8 teaspoons liquid smoke
- 4 beef bouillon cubes

- 8 racks pork baby back ribs (about 12 pounds)
- 1 cup hickory wood chips (optional)
- Barbecue sauce for serving

1. To make the barbecue paste: Combine all the spices and the brown sugar in a small bowl and set aside.

2. Combine the remaining paste ingredients in a medium saucepan and cook over medium-low heat, stirring occasionally, until the bouillon cubes dissolve, 3 to 5 minutes. Slowly add the spice mixture, stirring constantly, until thoroughly combined. Remove from the heat and set aside for 5 minutes to cool.

3. Thoroughly rub the ribs with the paste. Place the ribs in a deep, wide pan, cover with plastic wrap, and refrigerate for at least 5 hours or overnight. If you have any barbeque paste left over, cover and refrigerate it.

4. Prepare a fire in a charcoal grill (see page 10). If using the hickory chips, soak them in water to cover. When the coals are at medium-low heat, drain the chips (if using) and sprinkle half of them over the coals. Place the ribs on the cooking rack, cover the grill, partially open the vents, and cook for 30 to 40 minutes, turning frequently. Sprinkle the remaining hickory chips over the coals after 20 minutes.

5. Remove the ribs from the grill and serve dry or with a favorite barbecue sauce on the side.

Serves 10 to 12

Love That Kabob

Fifties kabob mania inspired a world of sultry marinades and skewered things, all twisted together with that essential aroma: eau de Kabob. These babies, also known as Annie's Lambies, were created by Lisa Shara Hall's best friend and mother, the late Ann Levy. In a moment of inspired creativity, Levy fueled her marinade with an intense hit of allspice that blasts through the meat, creating a tangy Armenian edge.

When preparing the skewers for the grill, it's best to thread the vegetables separately from the meat, so each component has its own smoky flavor. Serve with a side of steaming hot rice and plenty of watermelon wedges – and, to fully round out your Proustian back porch experience, a Mounds Sundae (page 89).

Marinade
- ¼ cup ground allspice
- 1 cup olive oil
- ¾ cup red wine vinegar
- 1 garlic clove, minced
- 1 small onion, thinly sliced

- 1 pound boneless lamb, cut into 1-inch-square cubes
- 12 mushroom caps
- 12 cherry tomatoes
- 2 small Japanese eggplants, cut into 1-inch pieces
- 1 onion, cut into 1-inch wedges

1. Combine the marinade ingredients in a medium bowl. Add the lamb cubes and cover. Refrigerate for 6 hours or overnight.

2. Prepare a fire in a charcoal grill (see page 10).

3. Remove the meat from the refrigerator

and let it
sit at room
temperature
while the
coals are heat-
ing. Pour off the
marinade and
reserve.

4. Thread the lamb cubes on 4 metal skewers. Thread the veg-etables on 4 separate metal skewers, alternating the veg-etables.

5. When the coals are medi-um hot, grill the skewers for 3 to 4 minutes on one side for medi-um rare. Turn and grill another 3 to 4 minutes. Brush each skewer with the marinade at least once during grilling.

6. Transfer the skewers to a large platter or individual plates and serve.

Serves 4

Cracklin' Sugar-Charred

A serious backyard cookout calls for steak, the kind of barbeque that fills your lungs with the beefiest perfume around. Oregon's barbecue-beef baron Pat Simpson uses a sugar-and-spice rub that caramelizes on the grill and creates a crackling, burnt-sugar char without and a juicy, rare center within. (A steak cooked beyond medium rare is culinary malpractice; proceed into this territory at your own risk.)

For best results, cook the steaks over a charcoal fire. If the coals are very hot, the

Cowboy Steak

dripping sugar coating can cause flare ups, so the steak should be watched to avoid too much charring. Do not cover the grill; that makes steak taste baked, not grilled. Be sure to use tongs, not a fork, to turn the meat; a fork pierces the meat and releases too much juice. After cooking, remove the steak to a cutting board, let sit for a few minutes, then slice diagonally into slices about 1/4 inch thick. Serve with Dragonbreath Corn on the Cob (page 76), sliced ripe tomatoes, a lusty red wine, and crusty bread to soak up the luscious juices.

It's almost impossible to cook too much steak, but if you have leftover slices, turn them into steak sandwiches on mayonnaise-smeared, butter-toasted garlic bread.

Sugar-and-Spice Rub
- 1 teaspoon salt
- 1 teaspoon freshly cracked black pepper
- 1/2 teaspoon garlic powder
- 2 1/2 tablespoons sugar

- One 2- to 3-pound top sirloin steak, about 1 inch thick

1. Combine the sugar-and-spice rub ingredients in a small bowl.

2. Rub one side of the steak with half of the rub mixture. Let sit at room temperature for 1 hour.

3. While the steak is sitting, prepare a fire in a charcoal grill (see page 10).

4. Spread the remaining rub on the other side of the steak and let it sit at room temperature for at least 30 minutes.

5. When the coals are medium hot, grill the steak for 4 minutes on each side for rare, 5 for medium rare.

6. Let the meat sit for 5 minutes before slicing.

Serves 6 to 8

Mondo Bongo BBQ Chicken

The best barbecued chicken has rhythm and soul. It fires up the blood and mesmerizes a crowd like a blistering '50s bongo beat. This one has a tangy-sweet bite and a delectable sticky glaze. Serve with Spo-Dee-O-Dee Chips (page 75) and Sweet Heat BBQ Coleslaw (page 74).

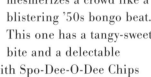

- 1 cup apricot preserves
- ½ cup Dijon mustard
- 2 tablespoons fresh lemon juice
- 2 tablespoons fresh orange juice
- 1 tablespoon minced fresh ginger
- 2 tablespoons soy sauce
- 1 tablespoon packed light brown sugar
- 1 frying chicken (about 3 pounds), cut up, or 3 pounds chicken parts

1. In a small saucepan, heat the preserves over low heat until just melted. Transfer to a bowl and combine with the mustard, lemon juice, orange juice, ginger, soy sauce, and brown sugar.

2. Light a fire in a charcoal grill (see page 10). When the coals are medium hot, move them to one side of the fuel bed.

3. Place the chicken on the cooking rack over the coals, skin-side down, and baste with the sauce. Cook for 5 minutes to sear. Then turn, baste, and cook the other side for another 5 minutes. Move the chicken to the other side of the grill, not over the coals. Cover the grill, open the vents, and cook, turning and brushing with the sauce every 5 to 10 minutes, until the juices run clear when pierced with a fork, about 15 to 20 minutes.

4. Heat any remaining sauce in a saucepan over medium heat. Bring to a boil and cook to reduce it by half, about 3 to 5 minutes. Transfer the sauce to a serving bowl and serve on the side.

Serves 4 to 6

Piña Colada Shrimp

W hy limit that fabulous '50s frou-frou combo of rum, pineapple, and coconut to a glass? Piña colada ingredients make a dynamite marinade for shrimp destined for the grill. If you plan to serve this with rice, try cooking the grains in coconut milk instead of water. You can also serve a simple salad of sliced pineapple mixed with minced onion and lime juice. But to really get the mood going, we suggest our Rum and Things drink (page 50).

- 36 medium-large shrimp (about 1 ¼ pounds)
- 1 cup canned coconut milk
- 6 tablespoons fresh lime juice (about 3 limes)
- 1 cup canned pineapple juice
- ½ cup dark rum
- 2 tablespoons minced fresh cilantro
- 1 garlic clove, minced
- Salt and freshly ground black pepper to taste
- Steamed rice for serving (optional)

1. Peel the shrimp and devein them under running water.

2. In a medium bowl, combine all the remaining ingredients except the rice. Add the shrimp, cover, and refrigerate for at least 1 hour or up to 5 hours (if it sits longer than this the lime juice will "cook" the shrimp).

3. Using a slotted spoon, remove the shrimp from the marinade and thread on metal skewers.

4. Prepare a fire in a charcoal grill (see page 10). When the coals are medium hot, place the skewers on the cooking rack and cook for 2 to 3 minutes on each side, or until the shrimp turn pink.

5. Serve with steamed rice, if you like.

Serves 4 to 6

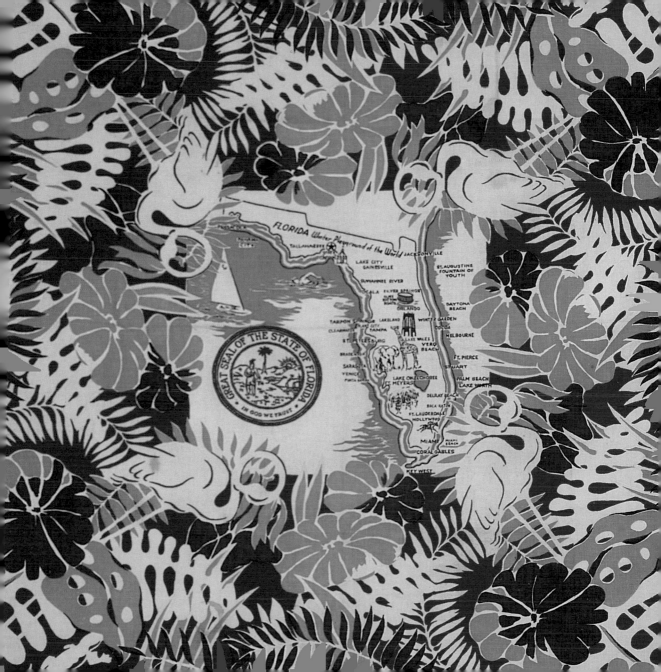

Grilled Tuna with Jamarama Pineapple Relish

The secret to superior grilled fish is simple: Don't overcook it. Tuna, for example, is best when the center is a little rare. Spoon on some sweet and sultry pineapple relish, and the dish really comes alive. If you're not in the mood to fire up the grill, broil the fish in the oven – it works almost as well.

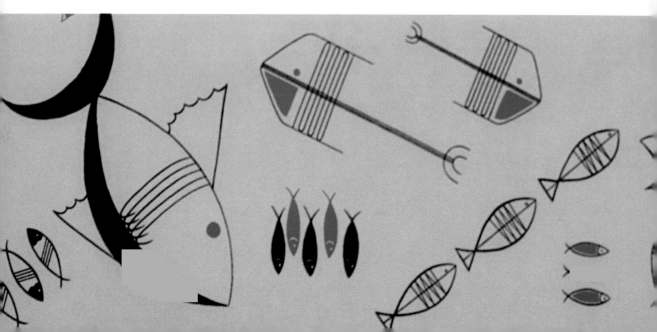

Jamarama Pineapple Relish

- ¹⁄₂ ripe pineapple, peeled, cored, and chopped, juice reserved
- 3 tablespoons minced fresh cilantro
- 1 small red onion, diced
- 1 tablespoon minced seeded red jalapeño chili
- 3 tablespoons fresh lime juice
- 2 dashes Tabasco sauce
- Salt and freshly ground black pepper to taste

- Four 6-ounce tuna steaks, each about 1 inch thick
- ¹⁄₄ cup vegetable oil

1. To make the relish: Combine all the ingredients in a medium bowl and set aside.

2. Prepare a fire in a charcoal grill (see page 10).

3. Rub the tuna steaks with oil and let sit at room temperature while the coals are heating. When the coals are medium hot, grill the steaks for 4 to 5 minutes on each side, or until the opaque on the outside and rare in the center.

4. Spoon some relish over each grilled steak and serve.

Serves 4

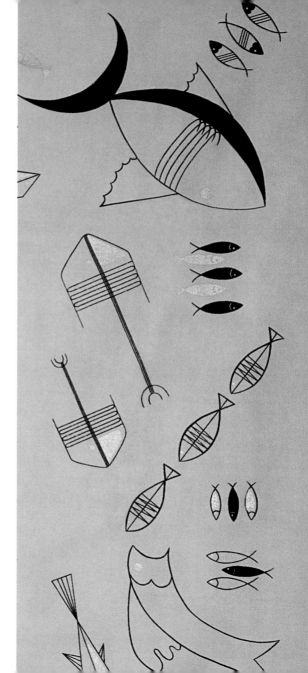

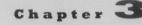

Chapter 3

Splish

Nothing, not heat waves, tropical rains, or a burger charred to oblivion, can undo the charms of a good patio drink. From fruity, frosty lemonade to thermo-nuclear cocktails, these beverages can be a pause for refreshment or fuel for spirited conversations.

Splash

SAN

Buzz-o-matic Coffee Cooler

C affeine on the rocks, packing souped-up cubes and a delayed power surge is the specialty of java philosopher Sara Perry, author of *The Complete Coffee Book*. You have a choice of floating-ice flavors, from chocolate-covered espresso beans to ice cream (see the following variations). Make to serve in chilled glasses.

What'll you have

Cool Cubes
- ²/₃ cup heavy cream or half-and-half
- ²/₃ cup sugar syrup (following)
- 16 chocolate-covered espresso beans

- 3 cups freshly brewed strong coffee at room temperature
- Sugar to taste

1. To make the cubes: In a small bowl, stir together the cream or half-and-half and sugar syrup. Pour half of the mixture into an ice cube tray and freeze for 30 minutes, or until the cubes have begun to set. Place 1 espresso bean in the center of each cube and cover with the remaining cream mixture. Freeze until firm, about 30 minutes.

2. Place 4 of the cool cubes into each of 4 chilled tall glasses. Pour ³/₄ cup of the coffee into each glass and serve at once.

Serves 4

COOL CUBE VARIATIONS:
Substitute a splash of Kahlúa for the espresso beans, or make a "coffee candy" cube by freezing a mixture of ²/₃ cup coffee and ²/₃ cup sugar syrup. Or, for high-octane cubes, simply freeze cooled freshly brewed coffee.

Sugar Syrup

Sugar syrup is a quick and effective ingredient that readily sweetens all kinds of drinks.

1. In a small saucepan, bring 1 cup water to a boil. Remove from heat and add ¹/₂ cup sugar. Stir until the sugar is completely dissolved. Set aside to cool completely before using. Cover and store indefinitely in the refrigerator.

Makes 1 cup

Butterfinger Express-o Malt

An arctic blitz of vanilla ice cream and a crumbled butter-crunch candy bar, with a malt-powder afterkick. Be sure to chill the glasses before filling them.

ENJOY
Outdoor Living

- 1 large (3.8 ounce) Butterfinger candy bar, broken into pieces
- 2 heaping scoops vanilla ice cream
- 2/3 cup cold milk
- 2 teaspoons malted milk powder plus more as needed
- 1 tablespoon espresso powder plus more as needed

1. Pulverize the Butterfinger bar in a blender. Measure out 6 heaping tablespoons and set the remaining candy aside.

2. Place the 6 heaping tablespoons back in the blender and add all the remaining ingredients. Blend until thick and smooth. Taste and adjust the flavors, adding more Butterfinger, malted milk powder, and espresso powder as desired. Pour into 2 chilled glasses and serve immediately.

Serves 2

VARIATION: Replace the Butterfinger with a 2.8-ounce Heath Bar.

Summer Camp Shake

This is the kind of frozen wonder you dreamed of at mess hall – a rare opportunity to rewrite childhood memories.

- 1 2.8 ounce Heath Bar, broken into pieces
- 2 heaping scoops chocolate ice cream
- 2/3 cup cold milk
- 1 teaspoon cinnamon
- 1 teaspoon vanilla extract

1. Pulverize the Heath Bar in a blender. Add all the remaining ingredients.

2. Blend until thick and smooth. Taste and adjust the flavors, adding more cinnamon and vanilla as desired. Pour into 2 chilled glasses and serve immediately.

Serves 2

Razzleberry Lemonade

On a hot day, nothing beats a cold, frosty glass of sweet-tart lemonade. Our version includes the kick of tangy raspberries. If fresh berries are available, they make a slightly better puree, although frozen unsweetened berries will do.

- 10 cups water
- 1 cup sugar
- 1 cup fresh or frozen unsweetened raspberries
- 1 ¼ cups fresh lemon juice (about 9 lemons)
- Grated zest of 1 lemon

1. Combine 2 cups of the water and the sugar in a non-aluminum 3 ½-quart saucepan over high heat. When the mixture comes to a boil, remove the pan from the heat and set aside to cool.

2. Puree the raspberries in a blender. Strain into a small bowl to remove the seeds. Add the lemon juice, lemon zest, and raspberry puree to the cooled sugar water. Stir in the remaining 8 cups water.

3. Pour into a glass pitcher. Chill and serve over ice.

Serves 8 to 10

Atomic Cocktail

The best way to jump-start an evening: Spike a glass of liquored tomato juice with an explosive dose of lemons, onion juice, and hot pepper sauce. The final flash of horseradish will leave no doubt that you're serious.

- 1 ½ tablespoons fresh lemon juice
- ¼ teaspoon salt
- 2 grinds of black pepper from a pepper mill
- 2 dashes Tabasco sauce
- 3 dashes Worcestershire sauce
- 1 heaping teaspoon minced onion
- 1 heaping teaspoon grated fresh horseradish
- 4 ounces chilled tomato juice
- 2 ½ ounces chilled vodka or tequila
- 2 ice cubes
- Pickled asparagus spear for garnish (optional)

1. Combine the lemon juice, salt, pepper, Tabasco sauce, and Worcestershire sauce in a glass.

2. Press the onion through a garlic press to extract the juice. Add the juice to the mixture. Press the horseradish through the garlic press to extract the juice and add to the mixture. Combine with the chilled tomato juice; taste and adjust the seasoning.

3. Pour the vodka or tequila into an 8-ounce glass. Stir in the tomato juice mixture. Place the ice cubes in the glass and garnish with pickled asparagus, if you like.

Serves 1

Rum and Things

Sure they're campy, and that's why we love 'em. Rum drinks are cool, literally (they're chilled) and figuratively (the rum is an essential fuel for the cocktail nation). This one is neon-hued and comes complete with a citrus tang and a mellow, dark-rum undertone. We serve 'em up with fruit-skewer garnishes, but no one will call the culinary police if you pop a tiny parasol on top.

- 4 ounces chilled pineapple juice
- 2 ounces chilled orange juice, preferably freshly squeezed
- 2 ounces chilled fresh lime juice
- 1 1/2 ounces dark rum
- Splash of grenadine for color

Garnish
- 1 small pineapple wedge
- 1 small orange wedge, about 1 inch wide
- 1 maraschino cherry

1. In a tall glass, combine the juices and stir to blend. Add the rum and stir again. Add the grenadine and blend.

2. Place the fruit on a small skewer. Use the skewer to stir the drink and serve it with the drink as a garnish.

Serves 1

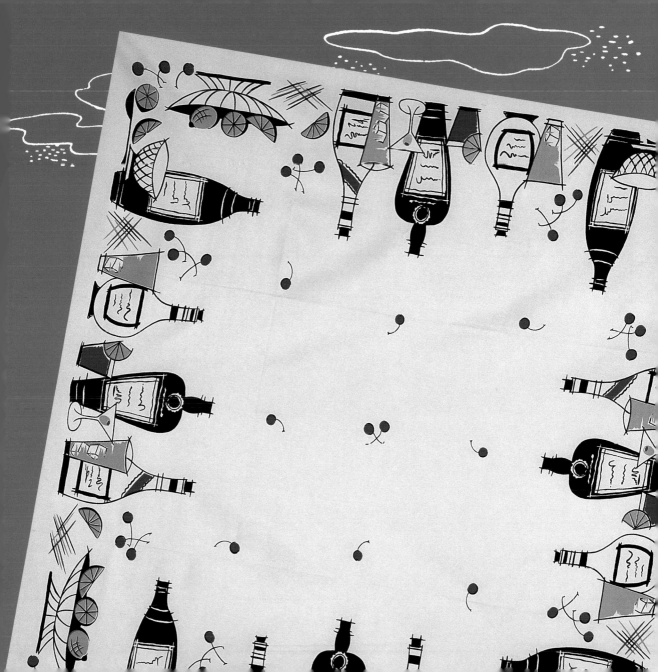

Maverick Martini

A great martini is a higher calling, a serious study of beverage aesthetics. It must be manly but sensual, subtle but slightly dangerous, with the power to seduce the innocent mind. This one strikes just the right balance between sin and satisfaction, with a touch of Scotch and a salty olive kick.

- 6 ounces gin
- 3 ounces vodka
- 1 ½ ounces dry vermouth
- Dash of orange bitters
- 1 teaspoon good-quality Scotch
- 6 anchovy-stuffed olives

1. Combine the gin, vodka, vermouth, bitters, and Scotch in a small pitcher.

2. Fill 6 cocktail glasses with ice. Divide the mixture among the glasses and top each with an anchovy-stuffed olive. Serve immediately.

Serves 6

Moon Glow Apricot Iced Tea

Form follows function in this arty cooler, which takes its character from apricot nectar ice cubes. As the cubes melt into the tea, they transmit a sweet fruity flavor. And they pack such an electric orange hue, you'd swear they glow in the dark. Remember to freeze the cubes in advance. If you want to use loose tea, replace the bags with 3½ tablespoons of tea.

- 1 can (46 ounces) apricot nectar
- 2 quarts water
- 6 bags Lipton tea, tags removed
- 1 lemon sliced

1. Pour the nectar into ice cube trays and place in the freezer. You will have enough to fill four fourteen well trays. Freeze until firm.

2. Bring the water to a boil in a large pot. Remove from the heat and add the tea bags. Cover and let steep 3 minutes for a stronger flavor. Remove the tea bags and let the tea stand until room temperature. Pour into a pitcher and chill until ready to serve.

3. Pack 8 glasses tightly with the cubes. Add the tea and garnish with lemon slices.

Serves 8

Chapter 4

Dagwood

In the '50s, the brilliant and the goofy came together ceremoniously between two sheets of bread. Some sandwiches emerged from department-store dining rooms, others from sweaty submarine shops and frenzied house-hold kitchens. And all sprang from an imagination unhinged. Let the sandwich building begin.

Redux

Hot-Iron Grilled Cheese Sandwiches

M aking a grilled cheese sandwich with a hot iron and aluminum foil may seem odd at first. But after you taste them, you'll agree that the weight and even heat of the iron produce the toastiest, crispiest cheese sandwiches on the planet. The rage in soul food circles in St. Louis, Missouri, during the '50s, they require little more than a side of Spo-Dee-O-Dee Chips (page 75) or Eat-Now Potato Salad (page 70), plus a pickle spear. Sure, you can use the fancy cheese found in food boutiques, or get healthy with sprouted-wheat bread. But to really taste the transcendent, there's only one way to go: thin slices of old-fashioned American cheese (yes, the ones wrapped in plastic) nestled between slices of white balloon bread. Open the foil occasionally while grilling to make sure the sandwiches don't overcook; when finished, the bread should be thin, almost flat, and beautifully bronzed, oozing cheese.

- 1 tablespoon soft unsalted butter
- 2 slices white bread
- 2 slices American cheese

1. Heat an electric iron to medium heat.

2. Butter one side of each bread slice. With the buttered side on the outside, make a sandwich with the cheese, leaving a 1/4-inch border of bread.

3. Wrap the sandwich completely in one layer of aluminum foil. Place on a counter or cutting board and weight with a hot iron. Leave the iron on each side until the sandwich is very flat and toasted, about 4 minutes per side. (Lift the foil periodically to make sure the iron is not too hot.)

4. Unwrap and serve.

Makes 1 sandwich

VARIATION: Replace the American cheese with thinly sliced Fontina cheese. Add a layer of prosciutto ham. Proceed as directed.

Chunky Chicken Salad on Toasted Raisin Bread

In homage to department-store dining-room cuisine, here's a serious chicken salad sandwich updated with orange zest and apples. The whole production is moistened with that high-IQ sour cream known as crème fraiche, available in natural foods and deluxe grocery stores. But regular sour cream can work, too. If raisin bread isn't easily found, add currants or raisins to the salad and serve the sandwiches on toasted white bread. All sorts of side dishes work beautifully, from a plate of crisp and crunchy vegetables to a pitcher of Razzleberry Lemonade (page 47).

- 4 boneless, skinless chicken breast halves
- ¼ cup good-quality mayonnaise
- ¼ cup crème fraiche or sour cream
- 1 tablespoon fresh lemon juice
- ½ cup finely chopped sweet white onion
- ½ cup slivered almonds, toasted (see Note, following)
- 1 Granny Smith apple, peeled, cored, and diced
- 1 teaspoon grated orange zest
- Salt and freshly ground black pepper to taste
- 8 slices raisin bread, toasted

1. Place the chicken breasts in a medium saucepan. Add water to cover and heat over medium heat until the water boils. Cover the pan and remove it from the heat. Let the chicken cool to room temperature in the liquid.

2. Cut the cooked chicken into bite-sized pieces and combine with the mayonnaise, crème fraiche or sour cream, lemon juice, onion, almonds, apple, and orange zest. Season with salt and pepper.

3. Spread one quarter of the filling on each of 4 bread slices. Top with remaining bread and cut the sandwiches in half to serve.

Makes 4 sandwiches

NOTE: To toast almonds, preheat the oven to 350 degrees F. Place almonds in a single layer on a rimmed baking sheet. Bake, tossing them once or twice during baking, until golden brown, 5 to 8 minutes.

Uncle Bob's Peanut Butter Sandwich with Texas Sweets

Sure, it sounds weird, but the combination of peanut butter, mayo, lettuce, and thinly sliced sweet onions creates something like an Indonesian satay sandwich. The lettuce adds that necessary crunch. Texas Sweets have a high sugar content, which makes them mild enough to eat out of hand like an apple. If unavailable, choose another variety that lacks the sulfur that causes the bite in most onions. Hawaii's Mauis, Georgia's Vidalias, or the Northwest's Walla Wallas have similar honeyed tones. Serve with a heap of salty potato chips and a big, frosty glass of milk.

- 3 tablespoons chunky peanut butter
- 1 tablespoon good-quality mayonnaise
- 1 ultra-thin slice of Texas Sweet or other sweet onion
- 1 lettuce leaf
- 2 slices firm white bread

1. Spread one slice of bread with peanut butter, the other slice with mayonnaise, and sandwich with the lettuce and onion. Cut in half to serve.

Makes 1 sandwich

Garden Grinders-A-Go-Go

Grilled vegetables, mingled with olives, sweet onions, and fresh mozzarella, create a swinging meatless version of a fifties favorite. For a slightly sweeter flavor, use half red wine vinegar and half balsamic vinegar.

- 2 Japanese eggplants, halved
- 9 tablespoons olive oil, preferably extra-virgin
- 2 red bell peppers
- 4 crusty sandwich rolls
- 8 tablespoons red wine vinegar
- 1 sweet onion, thinly sliced
- 8 ounces (2 balls) fresh mozzarella cheese packed in water, thinly sliced
- 12 large black olives, such as Kalamata, pitted and halved

1. Prepare a fire in a charcoal grill (see page 10), or pre-heat the broiler. Brush the eggplant halves with 1 tablespoon of the olive oil.

2. When the coals are at low heat (or the broiler is heated), place the eggplants and peppers on the grill (or under the broiler). Grill the eggplants until grill marks show on the cut side, about 4 or 5 minutes, then turn and grill on the second side for 4 or 5 minutes. Grill the peppers until the skin is evenly blackened, about 5 minutes on each side. (Follow the same procedure under the broiler.)

3. Remove the charred peppers and place them in a brown paper bag to cool. Close the bag and let the peppers cool enough to the touch, 10 to 15 minutes. Peel off the black skin with your fingers, remove and discard the seeds, and cut the peeled peppers into strips.

4. Split the rolls in half. Drizzle 1 tablespoon of the oil and 1 tablespoon of the vinegar on the bottom half.

5. Arrange an eggplant half on the bottom half of each roll. Layer each with one quarter of the roasted red pepper strips and a few slices of onion. Top each layer with a few overlapping slices of cheese. Press 3 olive halves into each layer of cheese.

6. Drizzle 1 tablespoon of the oil and 1 tablespoon of the vinegar over the top of the cheese layers.

7. Add the tops of the rolls and gently press down on them to slightly flatten each sandwich.

Makes 4 sandwiches

VARIATION: Replace the 4 rolls with 1 baguette. Split the baguette in half and sprinkle the bottom half with 4 tablespoons of the oil and 4 tablespoons of the vinegar. Arrange 4 eggplant halves on the bottom half of the baguette and top with the red pepper strips, onions, cheese, and olives. Drizzle with the remaining oil and vinegar, add the top of the baguette, and press down to flatten. Cut into 4 individual portions to serve.

Turkey Sands with Sassy

The beauty of a great turkey sandwich is that it fills so many needs: It's easy to make, and it's the perfect choice for everything from a picnic basket to a back-porch lunch party. And everyone from kids to food phobics likes them. This recipe is the brainchild of hot-shot San Francisco chef Lisa Cannelora. The layer of crisp apples tossed in vinaigrette adds a snap and a crunch — choose a variety that's juicy, crisp, and highly flavorful. The sage mayo adds a nutty, roasted flavor, but plain mayonnaise also works beautifully.

- 3 tablespoons apple cider vinegar
- 1/4 cup olive oil
- 1 1/2 to 2 teaspoons honey
- Pinch of salt
- Black peppercorns in a pepper mill
- 1 large crisp, tart apple, such as Granny Smith or Newton, cored and thinly sliced

Sage Mayo
- 3 fresh sage leaves
- 1 teaspoon butter, melted
- 1/2 cup good-quality mayonnaise

- 12 bread slices
- 12 ounces thinly sliced roast turkey
- 6 leafy lettuce leaves

Apples and Sage Mayo

1. Combine the vinegar, oil, honey, salt, and a few grindings of pepper in a small bowl. Taste and adjust the seasoning. Toss the apple slices with the mixture and let sit for 15 minutes.

2. To make the sage mayonnaise: Preheat the oven to 200 degrees F. Brush the sage leaves with the melted butter. Place on a baking sheet or and toast until crisp and dry, about 15 to 20 minutes. Crumble the leaves and stir them into the mayonnaise.

3. Spread the mayonnaise generously over 6 of the bread slices. Layer each with one sixth of sliced turkey, a layer of marinated apples, and a lettuce leaf. Top with the remaining bread slices, and cut each sandwich in half to serve.

Makes 6 sandwiches

VARIATIONS: The fresh sage may be replaced with 1 teaspoon crumbled sage. The lettuce leaves may be replaced with watercress.

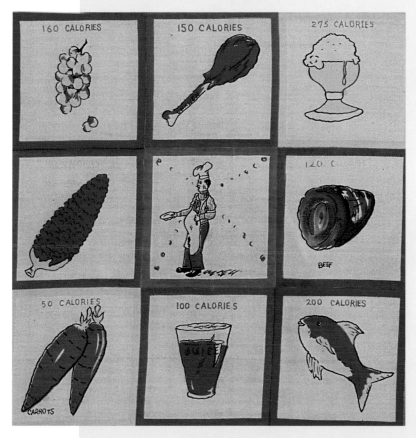

Date Nut Cream Cheese

Date-nut bread and cream cheese sandwiches evoke a time before a passion for the quick and the packaged broke our link with America's culinary past. Consider, then, the following on one of those days when a blazing sun, a baseball bat, and a few ants are all that's needed to get into the spirit of the proceedings at hand. With its deep vanilla perfume, the bread is the perfect coming together of chewy, sweet, and nutty. If you want a little more crunch, top the whole affair with slivers of crisp, tart apple.

Date-Nut Bread
- 1 cup coarsely chopped pitted dates
- $3/4$ cup (3 ounces) chopped walnuts
- 1 $1/2$ teaspoons baking soda
- 1 teaspoon salt
- 3 tablespoons vegetable shortening
- $3/4$ cup boiling water
- 2 eggs
- 1 tablespoon vanilla extract
- 1 cup sugar
- 1 $1/2$ cups unbleached all-purpose flour

- 6 ounces cream cheese at room temperature
- 1 large tart apple, cored and cut into thin slices (optional)

1. Combine the dates, walnuts, baking soda, and salt in a medium bowl. Add the shortening and boiling water, stir once, and let stand for 20 minutes.

Dee-lites

2. Preheat the oven to 350 degrees F. Grease a 9-by-5-inch loaf pan.

3. Beat the eggs in a large bowl. Add the vanilla, sugar, and flour and thoroughly combine. Stir in the date mixture, mixing just enough to lightly blend the ingredients. Turn the mixture into the prepared pan.

4. Bake for 45 minutes, or until the sides pull away from the pan and a toothpick inserted in the center of the bread comes out clean. Let cool completely in the pan on a wire rack.

5. Remove the loaf from the pan. Cut into 1/4-inch slices. Spread each slice with cream cheese. If desired, layer apple slices over the cream cheese. Serve open-faced, allowing 2 slices per person.

Serves 6

Chapter 5

Gimme

If you are in hot pursuit of those essential little dishes that can accentuate the essence of an outdoor feed, the following will help you meet the challenge. Don't stop with one! Serve several of these palate-popping counter-points at a sitting.

Remember, patio feasts are the cable TV of meals: The bigger the selection, the better.

Some Sides

Eat-Now Potato Salad

A novel twist on a classic favorite: chunks of potatoes mingled with a Caesar dressing fragrant with garlic and anchovies, then showered with grated Parmesan cheese. The dressing is so vivid and the cheese so pungent that the dish is a great power surge of flavor. Serve as a rousing accompaniment to grilled ribs (page 28), burgers (page 14), or chicken (page 24 and page 34).

- 1 1/2 pounds new potatoes

Caesar Dressing
- 1 large egg
- 3 tablespoons fresh lemon juice
- 1 1/2 teaspoons Dijon mustard
- 1 small garlic clove
- 2 anchovy fillets
- Salt and freshly ground black pepper to taste
- 1/4 cup vegetable oil
- 1/3 cup olive oil

- 3/4 cup (3 ounces) freshly grated Parmesan cheese

1. Cook the potatoes in a saucepan of boiling water until tender (about 12 to 15 minutes). Let cool, then cut the potatoes into 1/8-inch-thick slices. Place in a large bowl and set aside.

2. To make the dressing: Thoroughly combine the egg, lemon juice, mustard, garlic, anchovies, salt, and pepper in a blender or food processor. With the motor running, slowly add the vegetable and olive oils in a thin stream — the mixture will emulsify and resemble mayonnaise.

3. Toss the sliced potatoes with the dressing. Sprinkle the grated cheese over the salad.

4. Serve at once or cover and chill until ready to serve.

Makes 6 servings

Cheesy-Drippin', Garlic-Fumin' St. Louis Salad

W hat makes this classic Missouri salad special is the dressing, thick with shreds of Parmesan and ignited by crushed garlic. Combined with a nice selection of foods, some sweet, some biting, some oily, it makes a salad that's wonderful on a hot summer day with slices of crusty bread and ice-cold beer. To keep the salad extra fresh, serve it on chilled plates. To assemble it ahead of time, leave the onion out until it's time to dress the salad. If you're adventurous, roast the red pepper for a char-flavored twist (see page 63).

- 1 head well-chilled iceberg lettuce, outer leaves removed, torn into bite-sized pieces
- 1/2 Bermuda onion, cut into thin crosswise slices and slices quartered
- One 6-ounce jar marinated artichoke hearts, drained and cut into quarters
- 6 hearts of palm, cut into 1/2-inch-thick crosswise slices (optional)
- 1 small red bell pepper, seeded, deribbed, and thinly sliced, or one 6-ounce jar pimientos, drained and sliced

Dressing
- 2 tablespoons balsamic vinegar
- 1/4 teaspoon stone-ground mustard
- 1 large garlic clove, crushed
- 1/2 teaspoon salt
- Several grindings of black pepper
- 6 tablespoons extra-virgin olive oil
- 1/4 cup (1 ounce) freshly grated Parmesan cheese
- 1/2 cup (2 ounces) freshly grated Parmesan cheese for topping

1. Arrange the lettuce, onion, and artichoke hearts in a large serving bowl. Top with the optional hearts of palm and the sliced red pepper or pimiento.

2. To make the dressing: Whisk the vinegar, mustard, garlic, salt, and pepper together in a small bowl. Slowly add the oil, whisking constantly, until creamy. Stir the 1/4 cup Parmesan cheese and blend well.

3. Toss the salad with the dressing. Scatter the 1/2 cup Parmesan cheese over the top and serve immediately.

Serves 6

VARIATION: Replace iceberg lettuce with Romaine

Sweet Heat BBQ Coleslaw

Purists will tell you that a barbecue just ain't a barbecue without certain essentials: a great potato salad, monumental slabs of corn bread, and a good creamy coleslaw with a heap of crunch, a back-throat tang, and a sweet little blast of sugar. If you're looking for the real thing, pure and simple, this is it. Match it up with our ribs (page 28), burgers (page 14), or fried chicken (page 24).

Dressing
- 1 ½ cups good-quality mayonnaise
- 3 tablespoons crème fraîche or sour cream
- ⅓ cup distilled white vinegar
- ¼ cup sugar
- 6 drops Tabasco sauce
- Salt and freshly ground black pepper to taste

- 1 head green cabbage, shredded (about 4 to 5 cups)
- 2 carrots, peeled and grated

1. To make the dressing: Combine all the ingredients in a large bowl and stir well to blend.

2. Add the shredded cabbage and carrots to the bowl. Toss them well until thoroughly coated. Taste and adjust the seasoning.

Serves 6

Spo-Dee-O-Dee Chips

We dare you to eat just one of these rounds. They're hot and salty, crisp and crunchy, and absolutely irresistible.

- 6 tablespoons unsalted butter
- 4 baking potatoes, well scrubbed
- Salt and paprika to taste

1. Preheat an oven to 400 degrees F.

2. Line 2 baking sheets with aluminum foil. Place 3 tablespoons of the butter on each baking sheet and place them in the oven briefly to melt the butter.

3. Thinly slice the potatoes crosswise. Dip both sides of each slice in the melted butter and place on the baking sheets in a single layer. Lightly sprinkle the potatoes with salt and paprika.

4. Bake for 30 to 40 minutes, or until crisp and golden brown. Rotate the pans on the oven shelves midway through baking to ensure even cooking.

Serves 4

Dragonbreath Corn on the Cob

Fresh summer corn is a treat we crave every year as soon as the weather is hot. And grilling is absolutely the best way to cook corn: The smoky roasted flavor enhances the sweet corn taste. Here, a wicked hot pepper flavor combines with tart lime and sweet butter to dress the grilled ears. Yum.

- 6 ears of corn
- 6 tablespoons unsalted butter at room temperature
- 3 tablespoons grated lime zest
- 1/2 teaspoon salt
- 1/4 teaspoon cayenne pepper
- 2 tablespoons fresh lime juice

1. Clean the corn, stripping away the silk and husks.

2. In a small bowl, combine the remaining ingredients to make a smooth spread.

3. Spread each ear of corn with some of the butter mixture. Wrap each ear of corn in a piece of aluminum foil, covering it completely and sealing the ends.

4. Prepare a fire in a charcoal grill (see page 10).

5. When the coals are medium hot, place the ears on the cooking rack. Cook for 20 minutes, rotating the ears one quarter turn every 5 minutes.

6. Remove the foil and serve immediately.

Serves 6

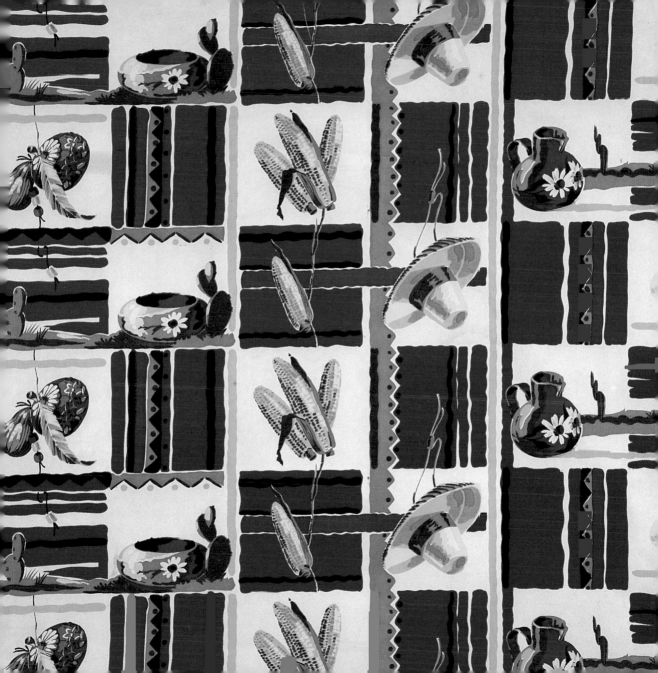

Back Shack Blueberry Corn Bread

- 6 tablespoons unsalted butter at room temperature
- 1 cup sugar
- 3 large eggs at room temperature
- 1 $1/2$ cups yellow cornmeal
- 2 cups unbleached all-purpose flour
- 1 tablespoon baking powder
- $1/2$ teaspoon salt
- 2 cups milk
- 1 cup fresh or frozen blueberries

Warm corn bread shot through with berries creates a contemporary Southern sidekick for grilled ribs (page 28), chili (page 16), or any other hearty dish. The cakelike texture is complemented by butter or honey.

1. Preheat the oven to 375 degrees F. Grease a 9-by-13-inch baking pan.

2. Cream the butter and sugar until smooth and fluffy. Add the eggs and beat thoroughly. Stir in the cornmeal just until combined.

3. Sift together the flour, baking powder and salt. Alternately, add the dry ingredients and the milk to the butter mixture in thirds, beating to combine after each addition. Be careful not to overbeat. Gently fold in the blueberries.

4. Pour the batter into the prepared pan. Bake until the corn bread is lightly browned and a toothpick inserted in the center comes out clean, about 40 to 50 minutes. Let cool on a wire rack before cutting into squares.

Makes fifteen 3-inch squares

Chapter 6

Sweeter

Why is life worth living? Certain things can get you through the rough times. The World Series . . . Chuck Berry records . . . *Twilight Zone* reruns . . . and dessert. Here they are, the chocolate numbers, the ice cream things, the grilled wonders that will add real substance to your day-to-day existence, not to mention a backyard bash.

Than You

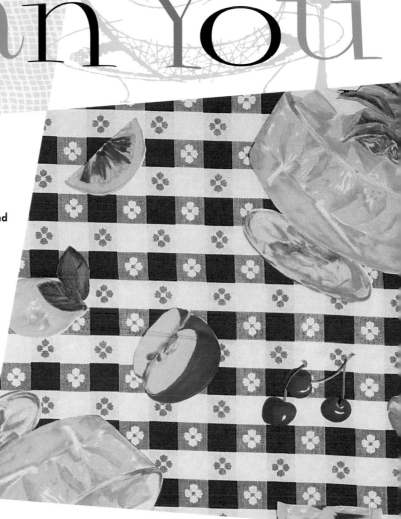

Big Daddy's Back Porch Chocolate Cake

No patio portfolio is complete without a great chocolate cake with a springy texture and a fudgy flavor that explodes in the mouth. This one's an archetype of the genre and all the better with a tall, frosty glass of ice-cold milk. The secret to super-moist cake is to beat the batter long enough to give it a glossy sheen. Serve this one plain or dress it up with powdered sugar.

- 3 1/2 squares (3 1/2 ounces) unsweetened chocolate
- 1/2 cup water
- 3 extra-large eggs, separated, at room temperature
- 3/4 cup plus 1 1/2 cups sugar
- 2 1/2 cups unbleached all-purpose flour, sifted
- 1 teaspoon baking soda
- 1 teaspoon salt
- 1 cup orange juice
- 1/2 cup vegetable oil
- 1 teaspoon vanilla extract

1. Preheat the oven to 350 degrees F.

2. Grease and flour a 9-by-13-inch baking pan.

3. Melt the chocolate in the top of a double boiler over simmering water. Remove from the heat and stir the 1/2 cup water into the chocolate. Set aside to cool.

4. Place the egg whites in the large bowl and beat at high speed until soft peaks form. Sprinkle in the 3/4 cup sugar, 2 tablespoons at a time, while beating at high speed, and continue to beat until the mixture is marshmallowy in texture.

5. In a medium bowl, combine the 1 1/2 cups sugar with the sifted flour, baking soda, and salt. Sift the mixture into a large bowl. Make a well in the center.

6. Beat the egg yolks. Pour the yolks into the well along with the orange juice, oil, and vanilla. Beat at medium-high speed just until blended. Blend in the melted chocolate, then fold in the egg whites. Pour the batter into the prepared baking pan.

7. Bake for 45 to 50 minutes, or until the top of the cake springs back when lightly pressed with your finger and a cake tester comes out clean when inserted in the center of the cake. Let cool in the pan on a wire rack. Cut into squares to serve.

Makes fifteen 3-inch squares

Grilled Pound Cake with Ice Cream and Caramel Sauce

When grilled over hot coals, slices of moist yellow cake are transformed into toasty miracles that exude a smoky almond perfume. You're really flying when you top the whole production with a scoop of vanilla ice cream and a thick dribbling of caramel sauce.

It's best to let the pound cake stand for 24 hours before slicing. If your grill isn't fired up, you can lightly toast the slices under a broiler or in a toaster oven. Or you can go the shortcut route: Forget about the purist police and buy the pound cake.

Pound Cake

- ½ cup (1 stick) unsalted butter at room temperature
- 1 ¼ cups sugar
- 3 large eggs at room temperature
- 1 teaspoon almond extract
- ½ teaspoon lemon extract
- ½ teaspoon vanilla extract
- 1 ½ cups cake flour
- ¼ teaspoon baking soda
- ¼ teaspoon salt
- 1½ cup plain yogurt or sour cream
- ¼ cup Amaretto

Caramel Sauce

- 7 ounces caramels
- 6 tablespoons heavy (whipping) cream

- Vanilla ice cream for serving
- Toasted almonds for garnish

1. To make the pound cake: Preheat the oven to 325 degrees F. Grease a 9-by-5-inch loaf pan.

2. Cream the butter and sugar until fluffy. Beat in the eggs, one at a time. Add the extracts.

3. Sift the flour, baking soda, and salt together in a mixing bowl. Add this mixture to the batter, alternating with the yogurt or sour cream and Amaretto in thirds. Beat until smooth. Pour the mixture into the prepared pan.

4. Bake for 40 minutes. Cover the top loosely with aluminum foil to prevent over-browning, and continue baking for 15 to 20 minutes, or until a cake tester inserted in the center comes out clean. Let cool for 20 minutes in the pan, then turn out onto a wire rack and let cool completely. Wrap in plastic wrap and let stand overnight or up to 24 hours.

5. Prepare a fire in a charcoal grill (see page 10), or preheat the broiler.

6. To make the caramel sauce: About 30 minutes before serving, place the caramels and cream in the top of a double boiler over simmering water. Heat until the caramels are melted, about 20 minutes, stirring occasionally. Keep the sauce warm over the simmering water.

7. Slice the pound cake into ⅓-inch-thick slices. When the coals are at low heat, lay the slices on the grill and cook until very lightly toasted and grill marked, about 1 minute on each side.

8. Transfer each slice to a plate. Top each slice with a scoop of ice cream. Drizzle warm caramel sauce over on the top and garnish with toasted almonds.

Makes one 9-by-5-inch loaf; serves 10 to 12

POUND CAKE VARIATION: Eliminate the almond extract. Add 1 tablespoon finely grated orange zest and substitute orange juice for the Amaretto.

SAUCE VARIATION: In place of the caramel sauce, top the cake with sliced fresh strawberries, sliced fresh peaches, hot fudge sauce, butterscotch sauce, or bittersweet chocolate sauce (page 89).

The Best Backyard Brownies You Ever Ate

A serious sin factor comes with this essential addition to the picnic basket or barbecue table. Thin and crackling, rich and chewy, chunked with pecans and perfumed with vanilla, these babies will take care of your weekly minimum requirement for chocolate. They're simple to make – this is one of those never-fail recipes – and they'll taste fresh for several days if tightly wrapped in plastic. If you want to cut the recipe in half, use an 8-inch square pan.

- 1 cup (2 sticks) unsalted butter at room temperature
- 4 squares (4 ounces) unsweetened chocolate
- 4 large eggs at room temperature
- 2 cups sugar
- 2 tablespoons vanilla extract
- 2/3 cup unbleached all-purpose flour, sifted
- 2 cups (12 ounces) coarsely chopped pecans
- Powdered sugar for dusting

1. Preheat the oven to 350 degrees F. Grease and flour a 9-by-13-inch pan.

2. Melt the butter and chocolate in the top of a double boiler over simmering water, stirring until smooth. Set aside to cool.

3. Beat the eggs, sugar, and vanilla until blended. Add the cooled chocolate mixture, using a rubber spatula to scrape out every last bit of it. Add the sifted flour and beat at medium speed until thick and smooth, about 3 minutes. Fold in the pecans using a wooden spoon or spatula.

4. Pour the batter into the prepared pan. Bake for about 25 minutes, or until a toothpick inserted in the center comes out almost clean. Let cool on a wire rack for 5 minutes.

5. Cut into squares. Pour powdered sugar into a sifter and shake a healthy dusting over the top of the brownies.

Makes thirty-two 1-inch brownies

Mounds Sundae

This is junk food gone uptown, and it's a beautiful thing on a hot night: vanilla ice cream balls rolled in big shreds of toasted coconut and topped with a bittersweet chocolate sauce. It's a cooling finish to a mouth-blistering meal.

- 1 ⅓ cups shredded coconut
- 1 pint vanilla ice cream

Bittersweet Chocolate Sauce
- One 3-ounce bittersweet chocolate bar, such as Lindt or Tobler
- ¼ cup half-and-half
- ½ teaspoon almond extract

1. Preheat the oven to 350 degrees F.

2. Spread the coconut on a sided baking sheet and toast in the oven, stirring halfway through, until lightly browned, 7 to 12 minutes. Let cool.

3. Place the coconut in a wide, shallow bowl. Scoop the ice cream into 4 balls. Roll each ball in the coconut to thoroughly coat it. Wrap each ball in plastic wrap and freeze until ready to serve.

4. About 5 minutes before serving, make the sauce: Break the chocolate into pieces and melt them in the top of a double boiler over simmering water. Add the half-and-half and the almond extract, stirring constantly with a wooden spoon until smooth. Don't worry if the mixture hardens and becomes grainy — it will smooth out.

5. To serve, unwrap the ice cream and place in serving bowls. Spoon 2 tablespoons of warm sauce over each ball.

Makes 4 servings

VARIATIONS: Serve the ice cream in little meringue shells purchased from a bakery. Or, garnish with coarsely chopped almonds or drained pineapple tidbits.

Lula's Luscious Little Banana Pudding Pie

One of the most soulful conclusions to barbecue comes down to this: layers of vanilla wafers and banana slices bound with a silky vanilla goo. This Deep South classic was passed down from Mamie Hammonds to her daughter Lula Barrett and on to you. It's so ambrosial that you'd swear this meringue-clouded beauty floated in from paradise.

- One 12-ounce box vanilla wafers
- 3 ripe bananas

Vanilla Pudding
- 2 large egg yolks at room temperature
- 2 cups milk
- 1 tablespoon flour
- 1/3 cup sugar
- 2 tablespoons unsalted butter
- 1/4 teaspoon fresh lemon juice
- Pinch of salt
- 1 teaspoon vanilla extract

Meringue
- 2 large egg whites at room temperature
- Pinch of cream of tartar
- 1 tablespoon sifted powdered sugar

1. Preheat the oven to 325 degrees F.

2. Lightly grease a 10-inch pie pan. Line the sides with vanilla wafers with the flat side of the wafers facing the center of the pan. Cover the bottom of the pan with wafers, flat-side down. Cut 1 1/2 bananas into thin slices and layer over the bottom layer of wafers. Cover with another layer of wafers. Slice the remaining bananas to add another layer. Top with another layer of vanilla wafers. Set aside.

3. To make the pudding: Beat the egg yolks in a small bowl and set aside. In a small bowl, combine 1/4 cup of the milk with the flour and stir to make a thin paste. In a nonaluminum 2-quart saucepan, combine the paste with the remaining 1 3/4 cups milk, the sugar, butter, lemon juice, salt, and vanilla. Cook over medium heat, stirring constantly with a wooden spoon until the mixture is hot. Transfer a few tablespoons of the hot mixture to the egg yolks and mix thoroughly. Pour the yolks into the saucepan and cook, stirring constantly, until the mixture comes to a boil and thickens, about 15 to 20 minutes.

4. Pour the pudding evenly over the top of the bananas and wafers.

5. To make the meringue: Beat the egg whites and cream of tartar in a medium bowl at medium speed until soft peaks are formed. Beat in the powdered sugar at high speed until stiff, glossy peaks are formed.

6. Spread the meringue over the pie and bake for 15 to 20 minutes, or until the meringue is golden brown. Let cool on a wire rack, then refrigerate until ready to serve. Cut into wedges.

Makes one 10-inch pie; serves 6 to 8

Dr. Bosker's Boogie-Woogie Brown-Sugared Barbecued Bananas

This recipe is your opportunity to go bonzo over bananas and create the perfect ending for an outdoor barbecue. This recipe is easily multiplied – grill as many bananas as you want at the same time. The entire presentation, from start to finish, takes about 15 minutes. When done, the bananas are soft, mushy, and wonderfully sticky, like caramelized banana custards.

- 4 unpeeled ripe bananas
- 4 tablespoons packed brown sugar or more as needed
- 4 tablespoons Grand Marnier or other liqueur of choice (optional)
- Whipped cream or ice cream (optional)

1. Prepare a fire in a charcoal grill (see page 10).

2. Place an unpeeled banana on its side on a cutting board. With a sharp, pointed knife, make a deep cut into the inside curve of the banana, through the skin and into the pulp, from top to bottom. The banana should not be cut in two, but the cut should be deep enough to permit the cook to spread the banana open slightly.

3. Spread the banana apart and pack 1 tablespoon of the brown sugar into this opening from top to bottom, adding more brown sugar if necessary to fill the opening. If desired, drizzle the liqueur over the brown sugar. Repeat to fill the remaining bananas.

4. When the coals are medium-hot, lay the bananas on the grill, cut-side up. Cook for 10 minutes, or until the fruit has soft-ened, turned a golden yellow color, separated slightly from the peel, and appears a bit caramelized.

5. With a spatula, transfer the grilled unpeeled bananas to plates. Top each with a dollop of whipped cream or a small scoop of ice cream, if desired.

Serves 4

Index

Equivalents

The exact equivalents in the following tables have been rounded for convenience.

US/UK

oz = ounce
lb = pound
in = inch
ft = foot
tbl = tablespoon
fl oz = fluid ounce
qt = quart

METRIC

g = gram
kg = kilogram
mm = millimeter
cm = centimeter
ml = milliliter
l = liter

WEIGHTS

US/UK	Metric
1 oz	30 g
2 oz	60 g
3 oz	90 g
4 oz ($1/4$ lb)	125 g
5 oz ($1/3$ lb)	155 g
6 oz	185 g
7 oz	220 g
8 oz ($1/2$ lb)	250 g
10 oz	315 g
12 oz ($3/4$ lb)	375 g
14 oz	440 g
16 oz (1 lb)	500 g
1 $1/2$ lb	750 g
2 lb	1 kg
3 lb	1.5 kg

OVEN TEMPERATURES

Fahrenheit	Celsius	Gas
250	120	$1/2$
275	140	1
300	150	2
325	160	3
350	180	4
375	190	5
400	200	6
425	220	7
450	230	8
475	240	9
500	260	10

LIQUIDS

US	Metric	UK
2 tbl	30 ml	1 fl oz
$1/4$ cup	60 ml	2 fl oz
$1/3$ cup	80 ml	3 fl oz
$1/2$ cup	125 ml	4 fl oz
$2/3$ cup	160 ml	5 fl oz
$3/4$ cup	180 ml	6 fl oz
1 cup	250 ml	8 fl oz
1 $1/2$ cups	375 ml	12 fl oz
2 cups	500 ml$_x$	32 fl oz

LENGTH MEASURES

$1/8$ in	3 mm
$1/4$ in	6 mm
$1/2$ in	12 mm
1 in	2.5 cm
2 in	5 cm
3 in	7.5 cm
4 in	10 cm
5 in	13 cm
6 in	15 cm
7 in	18 cm
8 in	20 cm
9 in	23 cm
10 in	25 cm
11 in	28 cm
12 in/1 ft	30 cm

Acknowledgments

The recipe for *Patio Daddy-O* was one part creative juices, one part eating and testing mania, and one part sharp editorial instincts. We are indebted to the following for sharing their time, culinary secrets, and support:

Our dream editor, Bill LeBlond, he of infinite patience and wisdom.

Associate editor Leslie Jonath and copy editor Carolyn Miller, two of the best pros in the business.

Ethel Fleishman, who has seen various members of this author team through four book projects and remains our trusted proofreader and arbiter of good taste.

Kirk Hall, for endless brainstorming, moral support, and eating stamina – the guy who is always there when everything breaks down.

Lynne Arany and Ink Projects for project development.

Joan Strouse, Ivan Gold, Mary Meyer, and Lena Lencek, for withstanding the rigorous tests of tasting and pot scrubbing.

To our esteemed friends, home cooks, and chefs who parted with their treasured back-porch recipes – Sara Perry, David Estes, Don Gronquist, Lisa Cannelora, Pat Simpson, Lula Barrett, and Rob Wolf.

And finally, to the memory of our dear friend, Ann Levy.